DEVON'S WILD FLOWERS

DEVON'S WILD FLOWERS

by T. Beer

VIEWING
DEVON
SERIES

JAMES PIKE LTD

St. Ives, Cornwall, England

(c) James Pike Ltd

First Edition 1974

ISBN 0 85932 082 0

Printed by Sawtell & Neilson Ltd
Newton Abbot, Devon

Some Devonshire Wild Flowers

Devon with its varying habitats has a wide variety of flora to offer those with an interest in the countryside at all times of the year. "Say it with flowers" is a well known expression and Devon says "welcome" to everyone, whether they are on the coast, moor marshes, woods, or the country lanes and riverside walks with which the County abounds. Without doubt the way to enjoy the countryside fully is to walk so please remember the Country Code and in so doing help others to enjoy the countryside also. Keep to Public Foot-paths and Rights of Way: close gates after you: do not leave litter about: control your dog if you have one: in a nutshell - consider others.

This book attempts to acquaint the reader with some of the wild-flowers he or she will expect to come across in Devon. Over 130 flowers are briefly mentioned and though this only touches on the subject it is hoped that the reader will be encouraged to find out more about the wild-flowers we all share the countryside with.

Coast

Devon's coastline is beautiful and varied, Dune systems and rocky beaches, sea cliffs affected by salt spray, pebble ridges and shingle, all providing a refreshing wild habitat for flowering plants.

Fortunately for us all such organisations as the Nature Conservancy; the Devon Trust for Nature Conservation and the National Trust are always active in preserving and conserving what is left of these habitats still unspoiled by mans sporadic expansion along the coasts and into the countryside. A typical reserve open to the public all the year round is at Braunton Burrows in North Devon and this has an extremely interesting flora.

Along tidal creeks and salt marshes a low growing gold coloured plant will be found. This plant, SEA PURSLANE (Halimione portulacoides) has silvery leaves which appear frosted, an effect caused by scales which reduce loss of moisture during hot weather.

A brownish violet coloured Iris called GLADDON (Iris foetidissima) grows on cliff slopes with bramble and blackthorn. This Iris has an unpleasant smell to man but attracts flies and beetles.

A common cliff plant growing in gay pint profusion is THRIFT (Armeria maritima). In early summer the rosy, honey-scented blossoms are found all over the County, the leaves remaining green all year round where the climate is milder.

The DOG VIOLET (Viola canina), the bluest of the wild violets blooms from March to June in open sunny spots, especially on coastal sand dunes and heaths. Ants often collect and store the ripe Dog Violet seeds.

At areas like Braunton Burrows, all over North and South Devon, one will find the SLENDER BIRD'S-FOOT TREFOIL (Lotus tenuis) with its longer more wiry stem than the commoner species. With narrow leaves and usually no more than four blossoms on each stem it is easily distinguished from BIRD'S-FOOT TREFOIL (Lotus corniculatus) with its richer colouring of yellow streaked with red. This brightly cheerful member of the pea family is often plentiful on sand, shingle and grassy banks throughout Devon. The plant has a lovely fragrance similar to that of Gorse when in flower and its name is derived from the fact that the long slender pods can be likened to the clawed toes of small birds.

There are several scurvy grasses to be found on the edges of salt-marshes in the spring and perhaps the most attractive of these is the LONG-LEAVED SCURVY GRASS (Cochlearia anglica). This particular species can be recognised by its long, tapering basal leaves. The flowers are white. The name comes from the fact that the plants used to be collected and eaten by sailors as a protection against scurvy.

From June to August the bright pink flowers of SEA PEA (Lathyrus japonicus, ssp. maritimus) can be found brightening the crests of shingle banks along the coast. The deep greenish-blue leaves are visible all year round.

Along shingle beaches at the level reached by high tides one finds the SEA KALE (Crambe maritima) a large conspicuous member of the cabbage family. An extremely hardy long-lived plant, the Sea Kale can grow up through masses of shingle after being buried by winter storms.

ENGLISH STONECROP (Sedum Anglicum) is a dwarf rock plant which spreads along the ledges of sea cliffs and sand dunes. When the white petalled flowers with pink undersides arrive, the greenish-blue leaves become red tinged. The ripe fruits are bright red in colour.

A common plant of rocks, walls and sandy ground on the coast and also inland is the WALL PEPPER (Sedum acre) also known as BITING STONECROP due to its acrid tasting juice. The bright yellow flowers are at their best in June and July especially on sand dune systems and shingle. The juice was once commonly used in the treatment of warts.

WILD CARROT (Daucous carota) is easily distinguished from its many relatives by its cushion-like flower heads. A strange and interesting lure to insects is a black flower often found growing in the centre of the white ones. This attracts the insects and thus ensures cross pollination.

A plant of sea-sprayed rocks is the pale yellow ROCK SAMPHIRE (Inula chrithmoides) a tall plant with golden flowers, not unlike asters, flowering from August until late autumn.   The foliage is an attractive glossy greenish-yellow.

On rocky cliff faces where the sea-spray reaches, one finds ROCK SEA LAVENDER (Limonium binervosum).   The blossoms are amethyst coloured and appear in July and August.

The pink flowering SEA MILKWORT (Glaux maritima) a member of the primrose family forms mats of spreading plants in grassy areas of salt-marshes and once established can survive extreme conditions.

A fairly common plant of the sedge family is the SEA CLUB-RUSH (Scirpus maritimus) which is not a true rush but as we have already said, a sedge.   A plant of shallow, brackish water and pools and ditches near the coast, it is often found in reed beds miles inland.   It would appear that as long as there is some hint of salt content brought in by tidal rivers this sedge will flourish.   Sea Club Rush stands from three to four feet in height, bearing their conspicuous brown flower-spikes in July and August.

A short, hardy species forming a mat-like vegitation along the stonier or sandy edges of salt-marshes in SEA HEATH (Frankenia laevis).   One finds its pretty five-petalled pink flowers blooming and expanding on sunny days in July and August and looking like mineature wild roses.

A plant of our softer mud-flats in estuary areas is the TOWNSEND'S CORD-GRASS (Spartina townsendii).   This plant does more to 'reclaim' tidal lands than any other and has been planted extensively for this very purpose.   Also known as 'Rice Grass' this plant is actually a hybrid of an American and English species, originally crossed and perfected on the South Coast.

STRAWBERRY CLOVER (Trifolium fragiferum), often mistaken for the common species, will be found growing in salty clayey areas of grassland near estuaries.   From July to September the seed-vessels are clustered in strawberry-like spheres which render identification a simple matter. The flower heads are an attractive rose-pink.

A late summer arrival is the SEA ASTER (Aster tripolium) a perennial wild blue michaelmas daisy with tongue-like leaves.   Bees and Butterflies are greatly attracted to this plants flowers. It is interesting to note that a variety has evolved without the blue ray-florets, leaving only the yellow buttonish flowers on the stems.

MARSH SAMPHIRE (Salicornia spp.) is one of several species of Salicornia growing in our salt-marshes. Members of the spinach family and collected in August for pickling this plants minute flowers appear in August and September. It may be interesting to the reader to note that Salicornias were also known as 'glassworts' and were collected in vast quantities and burnt, thus producing soda - ash for the manufacture of glass.

One will occasionally find the YELLOW HORNED POPPY (Glaucium flavum) growing on shingle beaches. Each large, bright yellow flower opens and withers in a day and appear throughout the summer. The crinkly leaves have a covering of silvery hairs and the long green horn-like pods give the plant its name. Bees visit the plant for its pollen.

Common in sand dune systems the deeply rooted SEA BINDWEED (Calystegia soldanella) has large trumpet-like flowers of a very attractive pink and rounded leaves. The flowers appear from June to September and are visited by bumble-bees, hawk-moths and certain smaller species of bee-fly.

A close relative of the roadside plant Bladder Campion is the SEA CAMPION (Silene maritima). Growing profusely on our shingle beaches and cliff edges, the white blossoms are at their best at midsummer.

SEA HOLLY (Eryngium maritimum) has suffered from overpicking in many places but the beautiful silvery leaved prickly plant survives in areas such as Braunton Burrows where, thankfully, it is preserved by the Nature Conservancy. The bright blue thistle-like flowers help to make this plant without doubt one of the loveliest of our coastal areas. A species of sandy beaches and dunes it attracts bees and butterflies throughout the spring and summer.

In complete contrast to the last named, the SEASIDE CURLED DOCK (Rumex crispus var. trigranulatus) is a tough looking plant with tall flower-spikes of green which grow up to four feet in height and later become a rusty brown colour. The fruits are triangular with three distinct tubercles. Curled Dock is common especially on shingle and sandy beaches in North and South Devon.

Similarly one finds SEA SANDWORT (honckenya peploides)

in these habitats, growing mainly in the zone at and just above high tide level. The spreading roots of this plant help to stabilise the sand. The flowers are greenish white and open throughout the summer.

On dry turfy areas of coastal dune systems will be found the CENTAURY (Centaurium erythraea) a member of the gentian family. From late June through to September the clear pink starry flowers appear on short stalks. Open during the day only, the flowers have a delicately sweet scent.

Another pink flower found in similar areas and in dunes where shell-grit is present is the REST HARROW (Ononis repens) a common sight in North Devon especially. Rest Harrows' long roots have been used as a substitute for liquorice in the past.

TREE MALLOW (Lavatera arborea) is a sturdy plant growing to ten feet or more in height on some of our coasts. The flowers are deep pink and it is said that a poultice made from the leaves has been known to cure styes.

Flowering in August and found near brackish waterways on estuarine areas is the MARSH MALLOW (Althaea officinalis). The flowers are rose pink, the leaves light greenish-grey and the plant was once used as a herb for the manufacture of a soothing jelly like ointment. This is also where the original 'marsh mallow' toffee came from.

LADY'S BEDSTRAW (Galium vernum) was a useful plant used for producing a substitute for rennet in cheese making. The roots also produced a red dye. The name is derived from the use of this plant as a bedding when people slept in straw, the plant having a pleasant scent. Though it grows all over the County it really flourishes on old dunes and sandy areas, producing masses of golden blossoms during June to August.

We cannot think of dune systems without mentioning MARRAM GRASS (Ammophila arenaria) with its wiry tufted leaves and white flower-spikes. This plant is the main builder and stabiliser of our dunes and spreads by runners through the sand often appearing to have been artificially planted.

Two other common grasses of our dune areas are SAND COUCH (Agropynon junceiforme) and SEA COUCH GRASS (Agropynon purgens). The former usually establishes growth on the seaward side of dunes whilst the Sea Couch Grass will be found on old dunes and also on the banks of estuaries where it is most common.

In habitats where shell-grit is found one will come across the CARLINE THISTLE (Carlina vulgaris) at many coastal areas as well as inland where limestone is prevalent. The brown and yellow centred flower heads are quite conspicuous and the plant also has pale green spiny leaves.

Common FORGET-ME-NOT (Myosotis arvensis) is often found on sand dunes and fields along the coast as well as inland. This plant is also called FIELD SCORPION GRASS because its stem is at first like a scorpions tail.

Marsh Habitat

The marshes and wetland areas of Devon are fascinating places, usually quiet places for lovers of solitude and the sounds of birds.

The large deep golden flower heads of the MARSH MARI-GOLD (Caltha palustris) is a common sight in this habitat and also found at the edges of wet woods and waterways all over Devon. These extremely beautiful flowers attract many insects including butterflies just out of hibernation.

As the cuckoos arrive in spring so comes the 'cuckoo-flower' or LADY'S SMOCK (Cardamine pratensis). Growing profusely in damp meadows these pretty pink flowers have cress-like leaves which are often used in salads. The Orange Tip Butterfly caterpillars love these leaves.

BOG BEAN (Menyanthes trifoliata) will be found along pond edges and bog pools in the county. The exotic looking pink and white starred flowers arrive in May and June. They are faced and fringed with fine white threads glittering like spun glass in the sunshine and this gives the lovely plant an unreal appearance.

RAGGED ROBIN (Lychnis flos-cuculi) is a common Marsh Campion with finely divided petals. From May to July this lovely deep magenta flower attracts many insects including bumble bees. Moths too are attracted by their delicate clove-like scent at night.

A small white buttercup growing in ponds, ditches and streams is the WATER CROWFOOT (Ranunculus heterophy-llus). The submerged leaves are thready but those on the surface are kidney-shaped and glossy above.

The wild iris or YELLOW FLAG (Iris pseudacorus) is a common plant along marshes and by pools and streams throughout Devon. This tall yellow flower likes plenty of

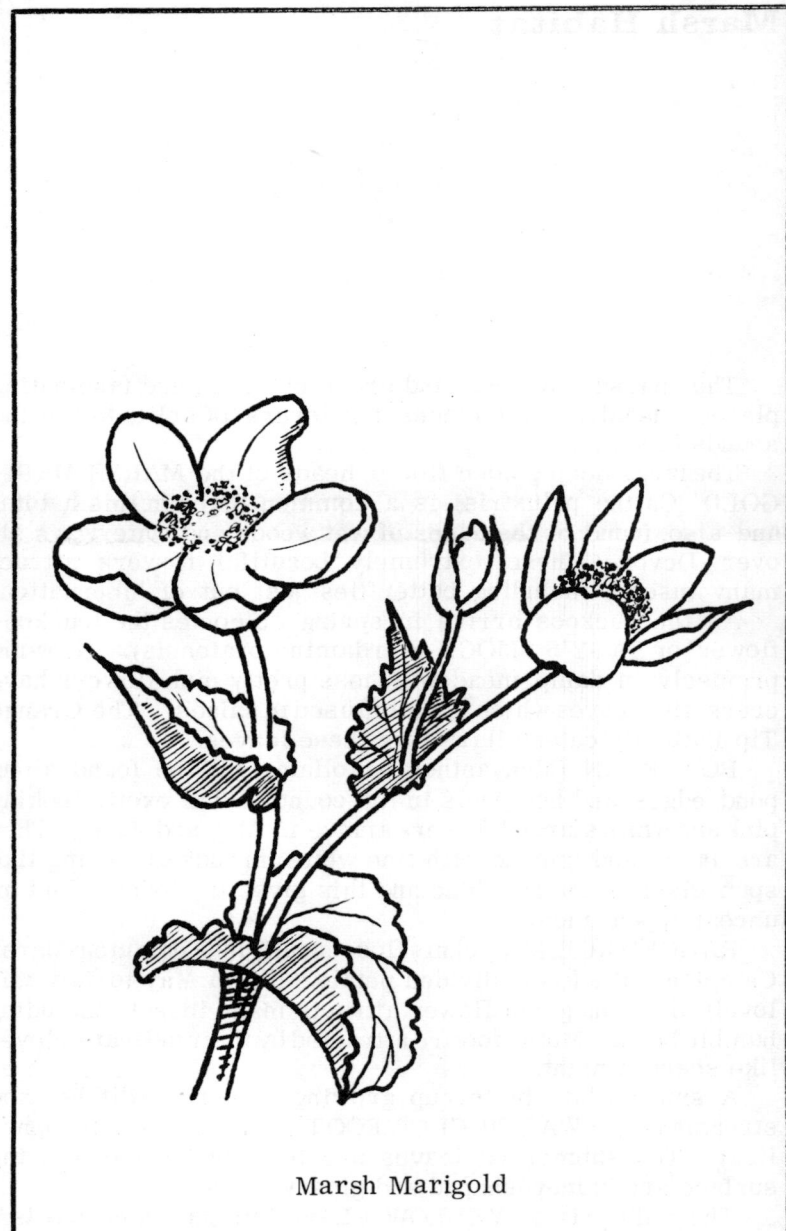

Marsh Marigold

light and therefore one often finds only the sword like leaves in shady places.

WATER VIOLETS (Hottonia palustris) are aquatic plants of the primrose family and flourish in pools and ditches in certain parts of Devon. One place I particularly remember is a marshy area near East Knowstone. The lilac coloured blossoms have deep yellow throats and emerge above the water in May and June.

Bogland also produces the EARLY MARSH ORCHID (Dactylorhiza incarnata) and the COMMON MARSH ORCHID, the first flowering in May, a month before the other plant Usually flesh pink they can also be brick red, bright purple or sulphur yellow or white.

An unusual looking shrub of wet areas is the GUELDER ROSE (Viburnum opulus) with its circlets of milky white flowers, the outermost being quite the larger and infertile. Their heavy perfume fills the night air and attracts many moths. As the summer ends brilliant red berries appear and these are a food favourite with birds such as the winter visitor the Fieldfare.

A useful plant of watermeadows is the MEADOWSWEET (Filipendual ulmaria) with its creamy, scented flowers looking so lovely especially in July. An excellent food for livestock this one and also once used for making a drink said to cure stomach-ache.

The TUFTED VETCH (Cicia cracca) is a common climber in Devons rough grasslands and by roadsides. It grows to a height of six feet at its best in the drier marshes and the bluish-violet flowers are quite small. This flower is sometimes called "Mousepea" by country people.

Often growing with the earlier named Bog-bean one will come across MARCH CINQUEFOIL (Potentilla palustris). The small flower petals are dwarfed by the unusual deep red sepals that spread into a five pointed star.

Our commonest water-lily is the YELLOW WATER-LILY (Nuphar lutea) which tolerates fairly swift currents. The rootstocks are massive and once a hold has been gained and the plant is established it is difficult to remove and is known to obstruct navigation.

In still pools and lakes throughout the county one finds the WHITE WATER-LILY (Nyphaea alba) a beautiful exotic looking plant with large glossy green leaves which are purplish on the undersides.

Ragged Robin

One may still find the MARSH PEA (Lathyrus palustris) in Devon though drainage of land is reducing its habitats as this lovely amethyst coloured plant requires constantly wet or moist areas with, it seems, traces of lime in the soil. I have encountered it at Whites Moor near East Knowstone and at Braunton Marshes entwining the stem of reeds.

An interesting plant of lowland rivers that flow slowly is ARROW-HEAD (Sagittaria sagittifolia). Interesting, I think, because of its three types of leaves, some like blades of light green grass which stream and wave in the current, others oval and lying flat on the surface whilst the third kind are really arrow-shaped and emerge from the water on rich green stems. The pale unisexual flowers also grow out of the water, the mail whorls uppermost.

Sometimes confused with Rosebay is the PURPLE LOOSE-STRIFF (Lythrum salicaria). A tall brightly purplish-pink species colonising riverbanks, marshes with bare peat patches, and stream banks wherever the sun can reach directly to germinate the seeds. Three distinctly different types of flowers occur each containing stamens and pistils which assist cross-pollination by insects.

The pink flowering BOG PIMPERNEL (Aragallis tenella), a creeping plant of peaty soil is found around the edges of pools in bogs and often spreading on wet grassy areas that have been closely grazed by livestock. Again land drainage is a destroyer of this particular species.

MARSH WOUNDWORT (Stachys palustris) appears from July onwards in wet meadows and along the banks of streams and ditches in lowland areas. The flowers are light purple in colour and unlike the common Hedge Woundwort which is noted for its foetid odour the Marsh Woundwort has scentless leaves.

YELLOW LOOSESTRIFE (Lysinachia vulgaris) is a late summer flower of many Devonshire riversides. Not in any way related to Purple Loosestrife this plant is a member of the Primrose family. A yellow dye is extracted from the bright yellow flowers.

Common in areas with wet slacks such as at Braunton Burrows, North Devon's Nature Conservancy area, the MARSH HELLEBORINE (Epipactis palustris) is an orchid with pinkish white flowers. The leaves are rather broad and cupped at the base to collect dew which assists the plant in surviving periods of dry weather. Bees and Burnet moths visit this plant.

If one walks through wet meadows the lovely scent of lemon or perhaps eau-de-cologne will often waft in the air. This will be from the plant WATER MINT (Mentha aquatica) a plant with some uses including the making of tea from its leaves, a well known gipsy beverage. The late summer flowers are favoured by bees and butterflies and are purplish-pink in colour.

HEMP AGRIMONY (Eupatorium cannabinum) is a tall perennial common in various damp habitats throughout Devon and often growing in large clumps. The dull pink flower heads occur from July onwards and attract many butterflies.

Extremely common as an invader of river valleys and water meadows is the HIMALAYAN BALSAM (Impatiens glandulifera). This tall pink flowering plant scatters its seeds in typical balsam manner by 'exploding' its pods. The black seeds float on water and therefore spread steadily and surely. Bees and butterflies are attracted to this plant.

ORANGE BALSAM (Impatiens capensis) is a smaller plant than the last mentioned and has lovely flame-orange flowers. In streams, riversides and marshes one will find this lovely plant from May to August at their best. Favoured by Bees and Wasps, the white pollen from the flowers seem to coat the insects with flour.

Everyone knows the thick red-brown pokers of the GREATER REED-MACE (Typha latifolia) though many people confuse them with Bullrushes. From March onwards the white silky seeds are distributed by wind and thus the plant spreads throughout the countryside to colonise pond and like edges.

During September when other flowers are becoming scarce Nature provides the late bees, butterflies and hover-flies with another source of nectar in the form of DEVIL'S-BIT SCABIOUS (Succisa pratensis). This heliotrope coloured flowering plant is found amongst rushes in fens, bogs and other wetland areas.

Though not abundant, a widespread flower of marshes or damp meadows is the SKULLCAP (Scutellaria galericulata) flowering from June to September. This deep blue flowering plant arranges its flowers in pairs facing the same way, growing from the base of the dark green leaves.

WATER FORGET-ME-NOT (Myosotis scorpiodes) is the

true forget-me-not and widespread in wet shady places throughout Devon. Its stem often grows along the ground sending out runners.

Hedgerows

Hedgerows are an interesting habitat and full of life. Devon still has many miles of hedgerows though it must be said that far too many fences are taking their place. These can only have a detrimental effect on our flora and fauna and the environment in general. However, flowers we have in their millions so let us explore a typical Devonshire hedgerow.

On crumbling banks of clayey soil, from February to April, the golden 'sunburst' of the COLTSFOOT (Tussilago farfara) can be found. A common plant once used for making herbal tobacco it quickly colonises the edges of new highways.

The earliest of our Buttercups, the LESSER CELANDINE (Ranunculus ficaria) blooms very early in Spring and its shiny golden flower heads are surely known by all. The word 'Celandine' means 'Swallow-herb' and it is so called because it welcomes the return of these birds in the Spring.

From February to April we find the SWEET VIOLET (Viola odorata) along our hedgebanks. This is our only fragrant wild violet and both the flowers and the leaves are scented. The colour varies from deep blue-violet to purest white.

Near streams and rivers and along roadside verges throughout Devon we find the BUTTERBUR (Petasites hybridus) with its large heads of flower spikes glowing pale pink. This plant, closely related to Coltsfoot, produces extremely large leaves after the flowers have withered at the end of April and these often shade out other vegitation.

One of my own favourites is the beautiful pure white STITCHWORT (Stellaria holostea) found along quiet hedgebanks all over Devon. Thriving only in grassy places this lovely member of the Chickweed family enhances the countryside wherever it grows.

Widely planted in hedgerows, the BLACKTHORN (Prunus spinosa) also has snow-like blossoms arriving in March. The blue-black sloes, the fruit of this spiny shrub, are rather sour but nonetheless pleasant in Sloe Wine. The country walker will find a blackthorn walking stick a boon companion and unbeatable value.

'Birds-eyes' as GERMANDER SPEEDWELLS (Veronica Chamaedrys) are very common in the hedgebanks and grass verges from March to June. This lovely blue flower will spread quickly and survive for many years. Attractive to bees and other insects despite the flowers small size, this speedwell opens for only a short period of time and soon drops off after being visited by the insects.

A favourite with children is the shiny arrow-headed CUCKOO PINT, (Arum maculatum) a greenish coloured wild arum also known as 'Lords and Ladies' or 'Parsons in the Pulpit' for obvious reasons. The leaves are often spotted with purple, arriving in April and dying away during June leaving spikes of green berries which when ripe turn scarlet. The entire plant is poisonous and one old country tale in Devon is that Vipers or Adders used to eat the red berries to obtain the poison for their fangs.

Plentiful in April and May the DANDELION (Taraxacum officinale) is often derided as a flower but take a longer look. They are really lovely and also have their uses. Their roots can be roasted and used as a substitute for Coffee, the leaves, though bitter, are good in salads and Dandelion Wine is excellent.

My own favourite flower of spring-time is the delicate pale yellow PRIMROSE (Primula vulgaris). Common throughout Devon thanks to a relatively moist climate these lovely, wonderfully scented flowers are much persecuted by indiscriminate for profit. Let us leave our flowers where we can all enjoy them - where they are growing.

To those who enjoy the natural foods of the countryside, the nut-flavoured roots of the COW PARSLEY (Anthriscus sylvestris) grows almost everywhere along hedgerows and roadsides. Also known as Lady's Lace it blossoms towards the end of May.

Anyone who has sat on a bank where WILD GARLIC (Allium ursinum) is growing will recall the onion smell of this very attractive plant with its white flowers. Also known

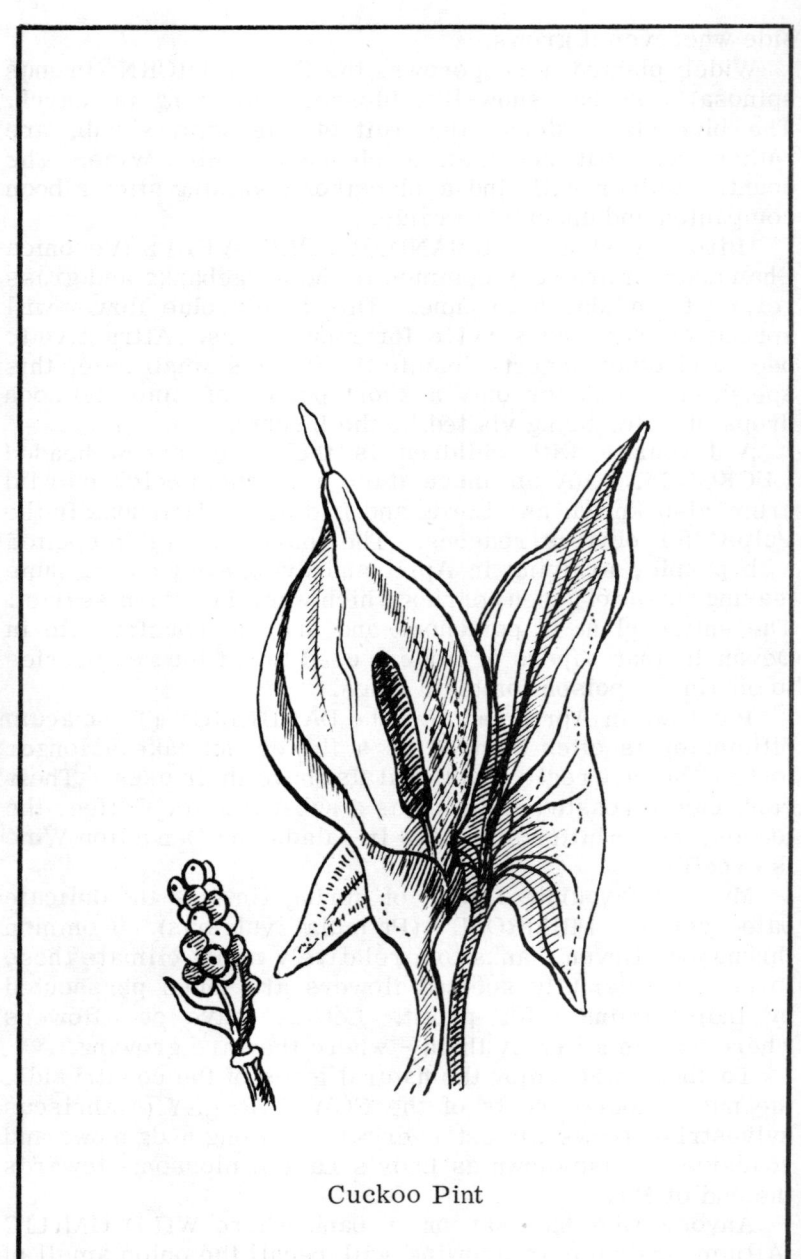

Cuckoo Pint

as Ramsons they appear in May and are common in woodlands and the typical Devonshire shady lanes.

RED CAMPIONS (Silene dioica) are abundant almost everywhere and vary from pale pink to deep magenta red. This is due to hybridisation with White Campions. Ladybirds hibernate in the seed pods of this plant during the winter.

Devonshire hill slopes are often blooming with GORSE or FURZE (Ulex Europaeus) and in April and May this flowering shrub is seen at its golden best.

On chalky soils and often elsewhere in the County can be found the DOGWOOD (Cornus sanguinea) a fairly common wayside shrub. June finds the white four-petalled blossoms in lovely clusters and these are succeeded by small black berries. Within the fruits is an oil that was once used for lamps, and the twigs and branches for basketry and tool handles respectively.

Sprawling and climbing over our hedgerows, the arching stems of the Dog Rose brighten the countryside in June. Faintly scented flowers vary from white to deep pink and scarlet fruit which ripen in December, known as 'hips', are favourites of the various members of the Thrush family. Rose-hip Syrup, rich in Vitamin C, is still a popular product of this plant.

COMFREY (Symphytum x uplandicum) a purplish flower, is often found along roadsides and greatly favoured by bumble-bees.

A conspicuous flower of roadsides and clayey pastures is the blue cranesbill with the large flowers, MEADOW CRANESBILL (Geranium pratense). Flowering during June and through to September it is a local plant absent from our coastal areas.

Flowering profusely from June until Autumn the BETONY (Betonice officinalis) is a showy deep pink plant of the mint family. Attractive to bees butterflies it has long been used for its medicinal properties. Flowers of white and pale pink are not rare.

Often blooming twice in a year the OX-EYE DAISY (Chrysanthemum leucanthemum) is a common flower throughout Devon. Also known as Moon Daisy, Dog Daisy or Marguerite, this flower is also common along railway embankments.

Common in damp situations is a tall slender thistle with reddish purple flowers. This is the WELTED THISTLE

Knapweed

(Carduus acanthoides) and its honey scented flower heads attract many insects including bees and butterflies.

The similarly coloured KNAPWEED (Centaurea nigra) grows in grassy places and is very common. Also known as Hardheads the plant is a great favourite with Goldfinches during the winter months.

In Devon, where woods and heaths have been burnt, and along railway embankments grows the willow herb called ROSEBAY (Epilobium angustifolium). Sometimes called Fireweed it is now well established and an attractive plant.

The GREAT HAIRY WILLOW HERB (Epilobium Lirsutum) grows up to five feet high and blossoms in July and August especially in the drier parts of Devons Marshes and is also common on the banks of clayey ditches. Honey Bees are attracted to the flowers of this plant.

The yellow CHARLOCK (Sinapsis arvensis) is now controlled by herbicides but was once a real problem in cornfields. Still abundant on waste ground and forming gay borders to our roadsides the Charlock adds a touch of colour to many areas.

POPPIES (Papaverrhoeas) were also a problem and now grow with the Charlock in many parts of the Country.

A beautifully scented flower is the HONEYSUCKLE (Lonicera periclymenum) found entwined in trees and bushes and always growing from left to right. The flowers attract hawk-moths and the red berries which ripen in August are eaten by birds. However a point to remember is that they are poisonous to man.

Bindweeds are common in Devon and the GREAT BELL-BINE (Calystegia sepium) is a weed of hedgerows, with large white trumpet flowers and bladder-like bracts beneath. A smaller variety grows in damp situations throughout Devon.

Another 'useful' plant is COMMON MALLOW (Malva sylvestris) found from June to September along roadsides and railway embankments and other similar spots. As a child I remember eating the 'fairy cheese' as we called the flat round fruits. The leaves are useful when applied to wasp stings.

In similar situations to the common Mallow we find the DARK MULLEIN (Verbascum nigrum) with pale gold blooms growing profusely up the stems. This plant flowers continuously from June to October.

YELLOW TOADFLAX (Linaria vulgaris) is a bright yellow

Rosebay

flower similar to an antirrhinum in appearance. The flowers are visited by bees and often give us a brilliant show of Autumn colour after hedges have been trimmed.

A plant often looked down on for no good reason is the IVY (Hedera helix) the well known climber of walls and trees. True, the shade of its leaves retards the growth of young trees at times but I feel that the plants' usefulness outweighs its nuisance value. Its flowers offer a large quantity of nectar to bees, butterflies, and wasps by day and moths by night. Blackbirds and Thrushes eat the berries at the end of winter and the plant also shelters many birds nests and provides roosts during colder weather.

HEDGE WOUNDWORT (Stachys arvensis) is a common hedgebank plant easily recognised by its claret coloured flowers and heart-shaped hairy leaves which have a rank smell when crushed. Also found in woods and shady places Hedge Woundwort grows up to three feet high and flowers in July and August.

A common plant of hedgerows made of natural stone and rock is the WALL PENNYWORT (Umbilicus rupestris) also known as Navelwort because of its leaves which resemble the shape of a penny with navel-like dimples in the centre. The leaves higher up the stems of this plant are more wedge shaped, almost ivy-like. Drooping greenish-white flowers appear in the summer on a stem of up to three feet tall.

Woodlands

Early Spring is the time of the Snowdrop and other apparently frail flowers, a point which has always amazed me. One finds the sturdier wild flowers such as foxgloves appearing so much later in the year.

SNOWDROPS (Galanthus nivalis), once called "White bulbous violets" are to be found in the woods of Devon as in much of western England. Beautifully white and fragile looking they nod their hanging heads and entice the hive bees and other early insects to sample their nectar.

WINTER ACONITE (Eranthis hyemalis) appears with the snowdrops. This golden and shiny flower is a member of the buttercup family introduced 400 years ago from Southern Europe.

A common shrub in our oak woodlands is the HAZEL (Corylus avellana) known by all for its lovely golden catkins and, of course, the nuts which ripen during October time.

An attractive plant of wooded areas, often found by the freshwater streams, is the PINK PURSLANE (Montia sibirica). This little flower originated in North America and is now widely established in the County. The flowers are normally pink, sometimes white, and appear in April through to July.

Another flower of Oak woodland and also associated with Ash and Beech woods is the LESSER PERIWINKLE (Vinca minor), a creeping evergreen found on clay or chalky soils. Look for the flowers in the sunlit glades of the woods. Brimstone and Small Tortoiseshell Butterflies are attracted to this lovely blue flower.

The WILD DAFFODIL (Narcissus pseudonancissus) is the native daffodil of England and can be found in the more open woods of Devon early in the year. As these golden

Snow Drop

flowers' bulbs are somewhat poisonous to livestock many have been removed from pastures.

The commonest violet growing in our woods is Viola riviniana, the common WOOD VIOLET. These lovely flowers are scentless and shed their pollen on the heads of bees, moths and flies when visited.

Carpeting our woods with white stars from March to May the WOOD ANEMONE (Anemone remorosa) is a familiar sight to country lovers. Open woodland is the best places to see these flowers which wither quickly after flowering. Bees are attracted by the pollen of the Wood Anemone, there being no nectar.

From May to early summer one will find the HERB ROBERT (Geranium robertianum) in woodland glades. Bright pink in colour or occasionally white this plant was named after Robert of Moleme, an eleventh century healer, its juice having powerful astringent qualities it was thus used for staunching wounds.

One of the deadnettles YELLOW ARCHANGEL (Galeobolon luteum) is common in old oak and ash woods on clayey soils. This pale yellow flower with its hooded blossoms is also favoured by bees.

Another common flower of moist clayey woodlands is the BUGLE (Ajuga reptans), normally blue, occasionally pink or white and attractive to bees and butterflies. May to July finds these flowers carpeting more open glades or where coppicing has taken place. Like Herb Robert this plant used to be valued for healing wounds and as a nose-bleed remedy.

At bluebell time we also find the EARLY PURPLE ORCHIDS (Orchis mascula) in bloom. The leaves are usually purple blotched whilst the flowers though gaily pink to deep purple in colour smells like cats. Another name for this flower is the "Cuckoo-flower". This is probably because the stamens of one flower attach themselves to a nectar questing insect and are thus carried to the next plant.

Another orchid, this time a much more inconspicuous plant is Listera avata or TWAYBLADE. Commonly known as 'double-leaf' this plant with its greenish flowers is common in clayey woods where some chalk is present. The two plantain-like leaves at the base of the plant give it its local name.

We can hardly mention bluebell time without mentioning BLUEBELLS. A really delightful sight is a deciduous wood

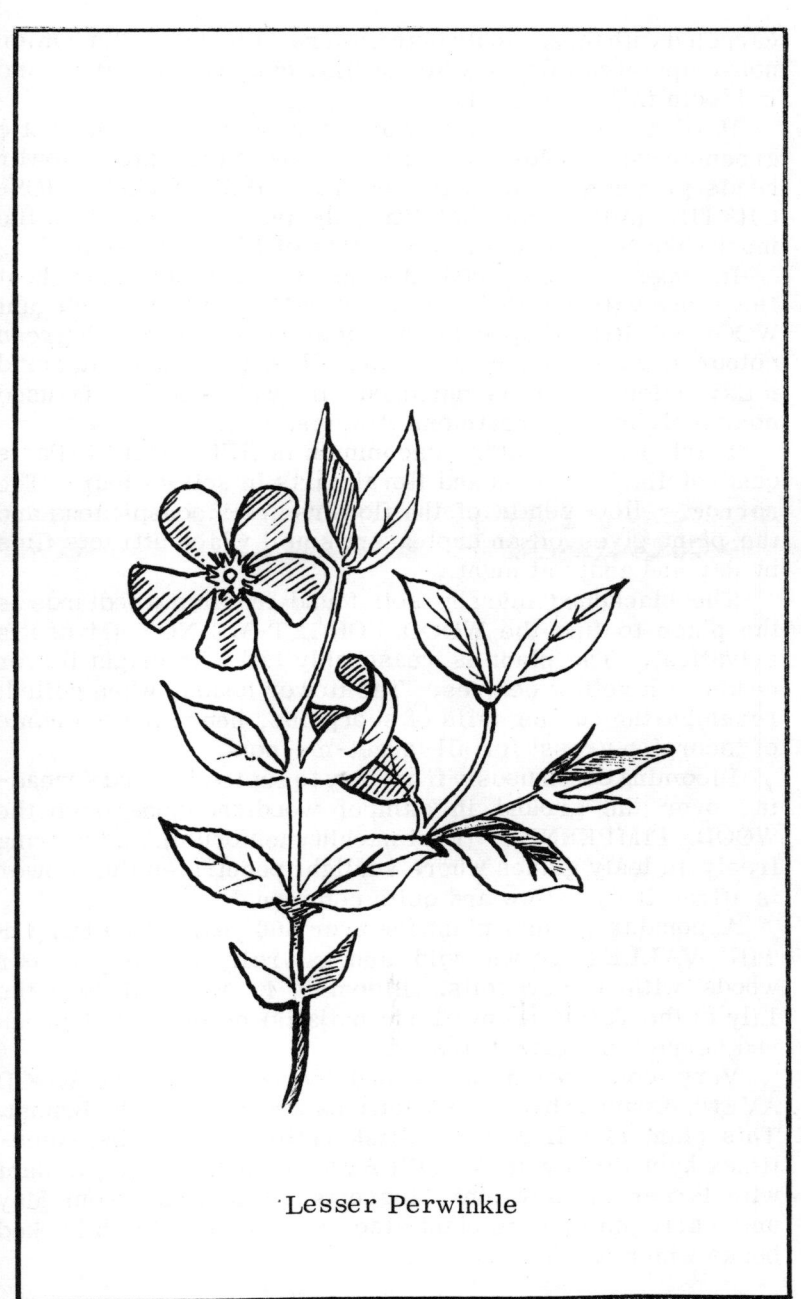

Lesser Perwinkle

carpeted with these richly blue flowers. Bluebells (Endymion nonscriptus) can also be white or lilac coloured and are found in bloom in May and June.

Hard to find but well worth the search are the little greenish-yellow Moschatel flowers, their four-faced flower heads giving them the name of 'Town-Hall Clocks'. MOS-CHATEL (Adoxa moschatellina) derives its name from the musk-like fragrance similar to that of Elder blossom.

In open or coppiced deciduous woodland throughout Devon one will find the greeny-yellow flowers of the elegant WOOD SPURGE (Euphorbia amygdaloides). The rich green colour is quite conspicuous and all spurges have an acrid milky juice which is poisonous if swallowed. It is used commonly for the treatment of warts.

Fairly widespread but uncommon is HERB PARIS (Paris quadrofolia) its leaves and floral parts in sets of four. The narrow yellow petals of the flowers are inconspicuous and the plant gives off an unpleasant smell which attracts flies by day and gnats at night.

The blackened marshy soil found in damp woodlands is the place to find the WOOD FORGET-ME-NOT (Myosotis sylvatica). The plant is reasonably tall with bright flower heads with yellow centres. The flower heads, when coiled, resemble the curling tails of scorpions, hence the old name of 'scorpion grass' for all forget-me-nots.

Blooming continuously from May to September and spreading over the ground in damper woodlands one finds the WOOD PIMPERNEL (Lysimachia nemorum). Flowering freely in leafy glades where sunlight penetrates this flower is attractively yellow and quite common.

A popular garden plant for over 500 years the LILY OF THE VALLEY grows wild and naturally in many of our woods with Limey soils. Blooming in May and June the Lily of the Valley (Convallaria majalis) produces poisonous red berries in some years.

Very common in our broad-leaved woods are WOOD AVENS (Geum urbanum) sometimes known as Herb Bennet. This plant is tall with smallish yellow flowers and some-times hybridisis with WATER AVENS (Geum rivale) a plant with larger creamy pink blossoms. Flowering from May until early summer the plant also produces fruit with hooked beaks which catch on clothing.

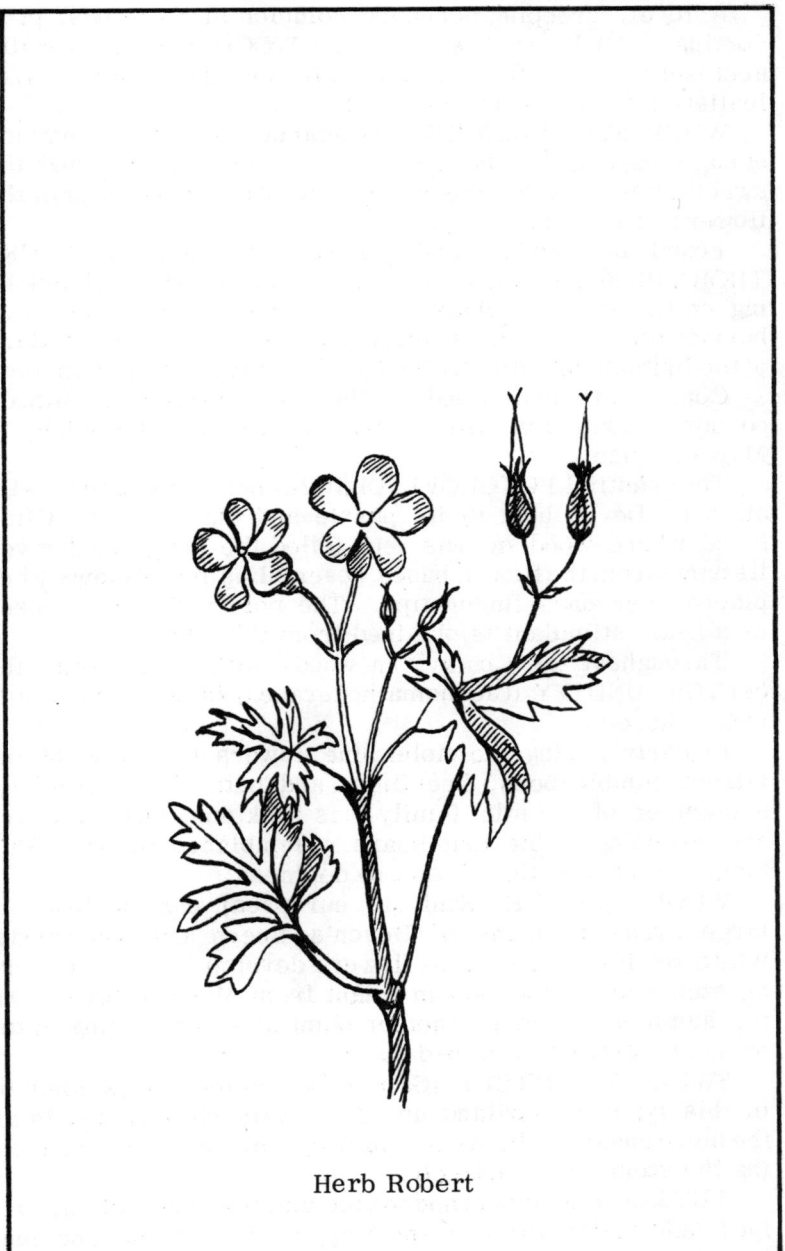

Herb Robert

A lovely creeping perennial common in old woods, predominately oak and beech, is the WOOD SORREL (Oxalis acetosella). The flowers are white and the Shamrock like leaflets fold downwards at night.

WILD STRAWBERRIES (Gragaria vesca) are common enough especially where the soil is more chalky and the sweet juicy berries are a favourite with birds. Again the flowers are white.

Found in both wet and dry woodland habitats, BUCKTHORN (Rhamnus catharticus) is a deciduous shrub flourishing on limestone or chalk soils. Do not eat the shiny black berries for they are extremely purgative. The caterpillars of the Brimstone Butterfly feed on the foliage in the summer.

Common in many woods is the RHODODENDRON (Rhododendron ponticum) with its purple flowers at their best in May and June.

The beautiful FOXGLOVE (Digitalis purpurea) grows wild all over Devon both in its purple and white forms. Often found where woodland has been felled the Foxglove derives its name from the flower bases resembling foxes claws when placed over ones finger-tips. The poison Digitalin, used as a heart stimulant is obtained from this plant.

Throughout the County, in woods with heavy soils, the herb GROUND IVY (Glechoma hederacea) is common almost everywhere.

In early spring the violet blue flowers are abundant and attract bumble-bees, bee-flies, and butterflies. Actually a member of the mint family it is its kidney shaped leaves and creeping habit that bears resemblance to Ivy. This plant was once believed to cure deafness.

WOOD SANICLE (Sanicula europaea) can be found in large areas in many of Devon's Beech and Oak woods. White or Pink, the small flowers develop in tight clusters on stems up to two feet in height from May and throughout the summer. This is another plant used for healing in the past and perhaps even to-day.

SWEET WOODRUFF (Galium odoratum) too is common in this type of woodland and this lovely white flower is all the more enhanced by its having the 'ruff' of leaves encircling the stem so attractively.

TUTSAN (Hupericum androsaemum) is a herb with charming bright yellow flowers which appear in late May and June in Devon. These develop into elliptical fruits which turn

Herb Paris

from green to red to black. The leaves were once wrapped around fresh wounds to heal them and has widely known healing properties.

WOODRUSH grows usually in the more acid soils of Oak woods or on moors where oak once grew. A common rush in Devon it grows to a height of three feet, flowering from May to June and usually found in tufts.

The three most common Buttercups in Devon are the MEADOW BUTTERCUP (Ranunculus acris); the BULBOUS (Ranunculus bulbosus) and the CREEPING BUTTERCUP (Ranunculus repense). The first named is the tallest, seen in damp meadows growing up to three feet in good soil. The stalk beneath the flower is smooth and the sepals upright. The bulbous species has ribbed stalks and a swollen, bulb-like stem base, usually flowering in May and June. Creeping Buttercup spreads rapidly by overground runners in many locations.

Perhaps the best known of our wild-flowers is often ignored in passing for the very reason it is so common. The DAISY (Bellis perennis) grows from wood edges all over our meadows, in fact in short grassland everywhere. Flowering almost all the year round this beautiful little flowers name is derived from 'Days-Eye' because it closes at night and during bad weather. One could liken this flower to a light-meter for it opens fully in bright sunshine and in varying degrees in varying lights.

Index

30	Aconite - Winter
20	Agrimony - Hemp
32	Anemone - Wood
32	Archangel - Yellow
19	Arrow Head
11	Aster - Sea
34	Avens - Wood
20	Balsam - Himalayan
20	Balsam - Orange
13	Bedstraw - Lady's
25	Betony
12	Bindweed - Sea
23	Blackthorn
32	Bluebell
15	Bog Bean
19	Bog Pimpernel
36	Buckthorn
32	Bugle
22	Butterbur
38	Buttercup - Bulbous
38	Buttercup - Creeping
38	Buttercup - Meadow
25	Campion - Red
14	Carline Thistle
10	Carrot - Wild
22	Celandine - Lesser
13	Centaury
27	Charlock
17	Cinquefoil - Marsh
11	Clover - Strawberry
11	Club Rush - Sea
22	Coltsfoot
25	Comfrey
13	Couch - Sand
13	Couch - Sea

23   Cow Parsley
15   Crowfoot - Water
23   Cuckoo Pint

30   Daffodil
38   Daisy - Common
25   Daisy - Ox Eye
23   Dandelion
20   Devils Bit Scabious
12   Dock - Seaside Curled
25   Dog Rose
9   Dog Violet
25   Dogwood

20   Forget-me-not - Water
34   Forget-me-not - Wood
36   Foxglove

23   Garlic - Wild
9   Gladdon
25   Gorse
17   Guelder Rose

11   Heath - Sea
34   Herb Paris
32   Herb Robert
27   Honeysuckle

29   Ivy - Common
36   Ivy - Ground

10   Kale - Sea
27   Knapweed

15   Lady's Smock
11   Lavender - Rock Sea
34   Lily of the Valley
19   Loosestrife - Purple
19   Loosestrife - Yellow

27	Mallow - Common
13	Mallow - Tree
13	Marram
17	Marsh Cinquefoil
19	Marsh Helleborine
15	Marsh Marigold
19	Marsh Pea
12	Marsh Samphire
19	Marsh Woundwort
25	Meadow Cranesbill
17	Meadowsweet
20	Mint Water
34	Moschatel
27	Mullein - Dark
17	Orchid - Early Marsh
32	Orchid - Early Purple
34	Paris - Herb
10	Pea - Sea
30	Periwinkle - Lesser
34	Pimpernel - Wood
23	Primrose
27	Poppy
12	Poppy - Yellow Horned
30	Purslane - Pink
9	Purslane - Sea
15	Ragged Robin
20	Reed Mace - Great
13	Rest Harrow
36	Rhododendron
27	Rosebay
25	Rose - Dog
17	Rose - Guelder
13	Sand Couch
12	Sandwort - Sea

11	Samphire
12	Samphire - Marsh
36	Sanicle - Wood
10	Scurvy Grass - Long Leaved
12	Sea Bindweed
12	Sea Campion
13	Sea Couch
11	Sea Heath
12	Sea Holly
10	Sea Kale
10	Sea Pea
9	Sea Purslane
12	Sea Sandwort
12	Seaside Curled Dock
20	Skullcap
30	Snowdrop
36	Sorrel - Wood
23	Speedwell - Germander
34	Spurge - Wood
22	Stitchwort
10	Stonecrop - Early
36	Strawberry - Wild
11	Strawberry Clover
14	Thistle - Carline
25	Thistle - Welted
9	Thrift
27	Toadflax - Yellow
11	Townsends Cord Grass
10	Trefoil - Bird's Foot
10	Trefoil - Slender Bird's Foot
36	Tutsan
32	Twayblade
9	Violet - Dog
22	Violet - Sweet

When visiting the

countryside please remember:

*GUARD AGAINST ALL RISK OF FIRE
  *FASTEN ALL GATES
*KEEP DOGS UNDER PROPER CONTROL
  *KEEP TO PATHS ACROSS FARM LAND
*AVOID DAMAGING FENCES, HEDGES AND WALLS
  *LEAVE NO LITTER
*PROTECT WILD LIFE, WILD PLANTS, AND TREES
  *SAFEGUARD WATER SUPPLIES
*GO CAREFULLY ON COUNTRY ROADS
  * RESPECT THE LIFE OF THE COUNTRYSIDE

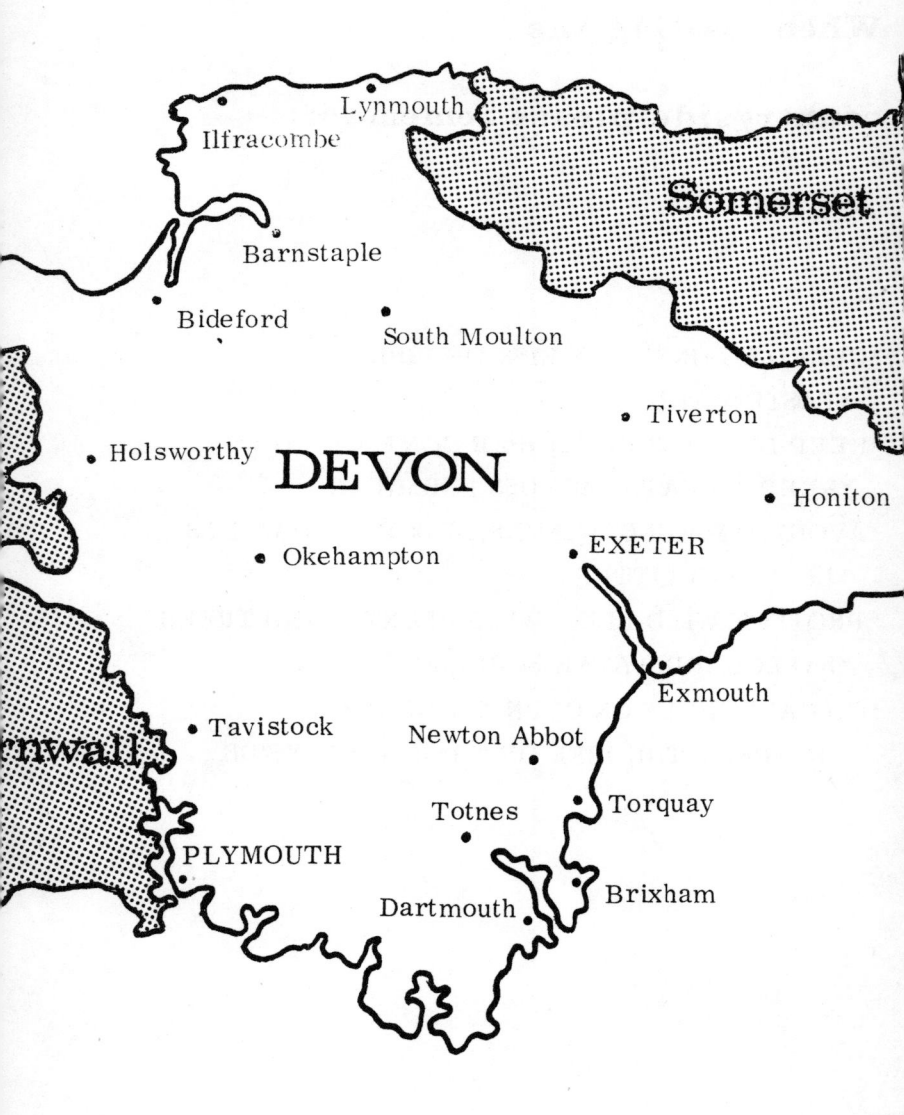

VIEWING DEVON SERIES

The following titles are available or in preparation

Devon's Best Beaches

Devon's Birds

Devon Car Tours

Devon's Castles, Gardens & Ancient Houses

Devon's Churches

Devon's Dartmoor

Devon's Fishing

Devon's Fossils, Pebbles & Shells

Devon's Ghosts

Devon's Legends & Folklore

Devon Long Ago

Devon's Northern Coast

Devon's Northern Footpaths

Devon's Railways

Devon's Southern Footpaths

Devon's Southern Coast

Devon's Waterways

Devon's Wild Flowers